Wonder, Ponder and All That's Yonder

Vaaruni C Debur

BookLeaf Publishing

India | USA | UK

Wonder, Ponder and All That's Yonder ©
2024 Vaaruni C Debur

Presentation by *BookLeaf Publishing*

Web: www.bookleafpub.com

E-mail: info@bookleafpub.com

ISBN: 9789360942267

First edition 2024

ACKNOWLEDGEMENTS

I would like to thank my parents; words cannot express how wonderful and supportive they have been, not just with this book but my entire life.

A shout-out to my English teachers at school who have always encouraged my writing and helped me step up my game.

Last but not least, to my incredible friends, who have stayed by my side through it all and also patiently and keenly listened to all my poems.

Thank you!

PREFACE

Growing up is easier said than done. Being the prime age at which everything starts to change and also the age at which friends are my heart and soul, I wanted to use my love for poetry and literature to share my day-to-day experiences and offbeat thoughts.

All said and done, this book talks about my early teenage years as an Indian girl and the little things in life that cause me joy, pain or both.

Teacher is Late!

Leaders are leading,
No one is following;
The teacher– no one wants to call.

The students are talking,
Leaders are struggling,
That one thing is clear to all.

The teacher is late!
Oh, what good fate
Has befallen the students of this class;

Shouting, 'Hey mate'!
Laughing we wait–
Our screams could shatter glass!

The teacher has entered,
Ready to mentor
And there we were making a fuss;

Only five minutes remaining,
We wanted to do something entertaining.
The amount of fun we had was stupendous!

Wishful Thinking

Ma'am is explaining about bills
But my dil* wants to sleep,
My eyes open I try to keep.

My mind wanders
And I start to wonder
At all the possibilities
Of me escaping this reality–

Into a world where Civics
Does not exist;
And days of fun and joy
Will not be missed!

Where ignorance of studies is bliss,
Marks don't matter at all;
Where straight A's won't be missed
If our studies take a steep fall.

How I wish this world was real!
But I'm stuck in Civics class.
No one cares about the Legislative ordeal;
Yes! The bell rang at last.

*dil – Hindi word for 'heart'

United Nations

The United Nations
Won standing ovations
After World War II.

The Allied Leaders
Stood with Churchill for freedom
And also dear old 'Roose'.

With Declarations and Charters
Like Moscow and Dumbarton,
Atlantic, London and more–

They have five different nations
And New York as their mansion;
All this at their door!

With aims and objectives,
Principles and memberships,
And their very own flag,

Six different languages
And various Councils–
They made sure to never lag!

Hope and Hopelessness

A winning team, on paper,
On the field, rather horrid!
Still, in our hearts, they resemble royalty,
And, without solid reason, have our loyalty.

A few promising starts,
Made it to the final too,
Though the cup has never been theirs,
'Yet' is a word we hold on to.

New season, same aim, same promise,
Our optimism gives way to gloom;
Defeating them has proven to be a challenge,
Once in a blue moon.

Despite the recurring let-downs,
We stay true to our word,
We cheer, curse and troll them,
And forgive them, though it seems absurd.

Happy Independence Day!

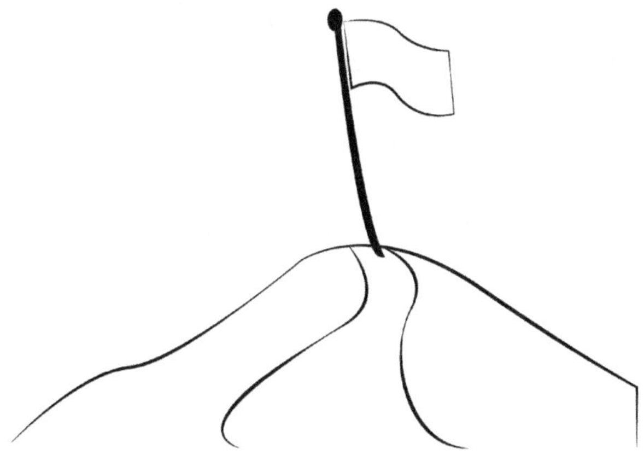

With the festive atmosphere comes a doubt –
Is this Earth or heaven?
The Tiranga* waved gleefully in the highest of
heights;
The date – August 15th, 1947.

The survivors' scars gave way to a deeper pain –
Pain in memory of the victims slain.
The soldiers, the fearless and the innocent alike
Fought gallantly with swords and silent strikes.

On this day,
They were reminisced with folded hands and a
smile,
For their sacrifices weren't in vain;
The people danced and sang, as they knew it
would be
A free country where their fellow fighters would
be born again.

Our country is free, it is our own;
The 'better tomorrow' they fought for is finally
today
So, from all the freedom fighters that made our
lives brighter –
A very HAPPY INDEPENDENCE DAY!

*The tricolour National flag of India

Fam Jam

Having a big family
Means the house is never empty,
And though I am a 'one-and-only' child,
I've got cousins aplenty!

Family functions are lively and joyous,
Whether you're seventy, seventeen or two;
Playing cards and singing together,
Seems like everyone can carry a tune!

Except itchy dresses and unknown aunties
Who somehow know your name,
The rest is quite enjoyable, especially the food,
Which is the reason everyone came.

Cheeks pinched and stomach filled,
I feel exhausted and content;
Pick yourself up, it's time for coffee and ice
cream,
The day's not over yet!

In the Mood for Food

You need to eat to live,
But do you live to eat?
Food makes both me
And my stomach feel complete!

Be it sweet or savoury,
Filled with cake or maybe gravy,
I shall relish it for sure,
And I shall always want more!

Of course, I too have dislikes,
Though they are less than few;
And if I'm feeling hungry,
Then a King's meal is due!

Right after eating,
I could have a second meal;
Any one of my many favourites
Is enough to make me squeal!

If you dare to steal my food,
Then enemy beware–
I shall hunt you down
For this is the one thing I shan't spare!

When it comes to quantity,
I eat without a care;
Yes, I'd be happy to finish the rest,
As well as my best friend's share!

Make or Break-Through

You don't need to fight it all,
Just need to be yourself;
Don't have to climb the wall,
Just break through instead!

If you didn't make the right call,
You can always put it on hold,
Though not for long, just
Until you're out of the cold.

You can be a storyteller,
Going from town to town,
Narrating tales and sights,
Turning frowns upside down!

Or you can be a pirate,
Taming the wildest sea,
And find the long-lost treasure
If that's what makes you happy.

Live, laugh and love,
So that when you get old,
You can gather your grandchildren,
And tell them how you found the gold!

Long Time No See!

Tell me Princess,
How do you do?
Walking by and stealing glances,
Wearing a glass shoe.
Face of gold; heart of black!
However, this secret is just known by few;
Tell me Princess, how do you do?

See you there shining, so bright,
Brighter than a sword in the dimmest of lights,
Ready to stab those around you.
Your fashion sense has stayed the same,
Your cunning nature remains unchanged,
It's about time the light shines on the truth—

Tell me Princess,
Where's your aura of smug?
Long time no see,
I'd rather a hug!
You had better reform and redeem,
And wipe away that pout,
For sooner or later,
The truth will out!

Home Alone!

Suddenly, it's silent,
Not a sound in the house;
I'm home alone!
I turn the music up loud.

Watch my favourite show,
Eat my favourite snack,
With no one to reprimand me,
Discipline is something I lack.

I put on a horror movie,
Not the best decision–
It's not the movie that scares me,
But rather the sudden hammering and car
ignition!

I get a call from my best friend
Which serves well as a distraction,
There's enough to gossip, like in a teen movie,
So lights, camera, action!

Ding-dong goes the doorbell,
I wonder who it could be;
I look through the peephole,
Were we expecting a delivery?

Far too soon, everyone's home,
And it's back to my daily routine,
My parents turn to me, rather suspicious,
For the house looks far too clean!

Holiday Joy!

It's the holidays!
It's jolly and like always
Filled with laughter and fun,
And much-needed freedom!

Books shut inside the cupboard,
Just the school ones, of course,
And marvellous weather too, what luck!
Wait, they sent us holiday homework?

No, it's not much,
Just a thirty-page project,
And counts for the finals too,
So really not that important.

Oh well, I'll work hard,
And be done with it; the sooner the better,
It turned out rather lovely too–
You can't be serious!
The break's almost over?

Truly Magical

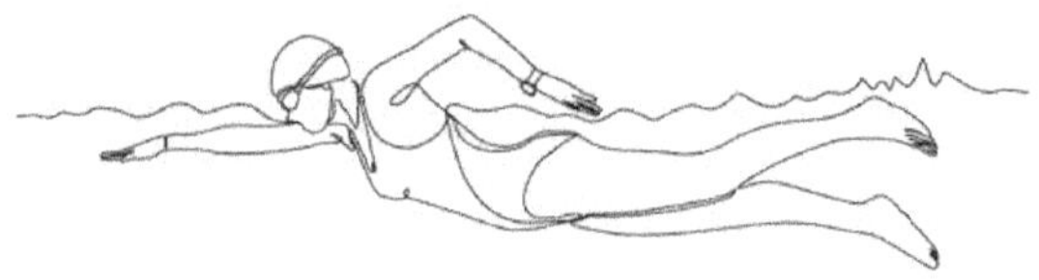

I jump in, never once hesitating,
The feeling – quite breathtaking;
The cold water gives the warmth of home,
Feeling neither scared nor alone.

Swim, and the troubles wash away;
Swim, what a way to spend the day!
Swim, and forevermore I would,
For I would live underwater if I could.

When I'm in the water, I have no doubt
There's a fire in me, nothing could ever put out!
Be it a sunny morning or a chilly night,
I shall swim if there's a pool in sight.

I climb out, a smile on my face,
For me, this is the truly magical space,
Surrounded by water, fun abundant,
I return, feeling triumphant!

The Story of Friendship Day

This is the story of a fight
Between a binder clip and a dictionary –
The cause of anger was light,
Yet they waged war, neither one wary.

This is a story of horror!
When the dictionary fell apart –
It was stuck with glue, and out of the few
The binder was chosen to hold together its parts.

This is a story of surprise!
As the sworn enemies began to get along –
The binder shooed the hungry mice,
In return, his grammar was spot on!

This is a story of friendship
Which blossomed from passionate hate;
And this is why we celebrate
Friendship Day on this date!

Imagine This:

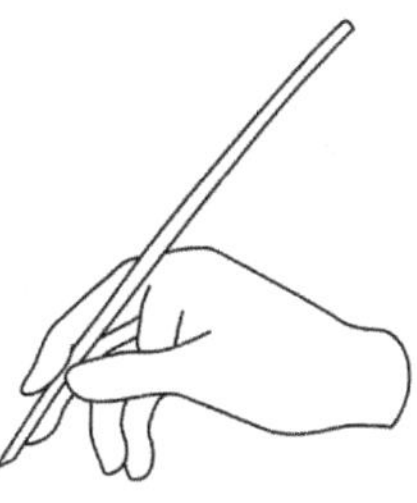

First breath of fresh air,
First look at the world,
First swell of pride
At the name to uphold.

First look of awe
At the perfection of others;
The realisation that none, so to speak,
Have ruffled feathers.

But, uh-oh, what's this?
A simple miscalculation –
With an arm instead of a leg,
You get all the attention.

That's when you see it –
First sight of your doom;
You look up, eyes filled with terror,
Ever closer it looms.

At this moment, you realise,
While praying for God's grace,
That this is probably what a word
Feels like to be erased.

Summer Bummer

Summer break's a blast!
But how long will the fun last?
It feels good to be free,
But how good can it be?

A few weeks in
The excitement wears off,
Boredom is a sin
Whose culprit, to catch, is tough.

Many shows – same story;
Many friends – searching for glory;
And all that I used to adore
Has turned into quite a bore.

Summer break's a blast,
Just until the fun lasts;
It feels good to be free,
As does running, till you scrape your knee.

(T)Rain of Thought

It had been a while,
But just the same,
The rain pattered on the window pane –
Loving but harsh,
With sorrow and glee –
Seemingly relieved to, at last, be free!

But what secrets does it have to hide?
I wonder,
As I watch from the warmth of inside.
Every drop tells a mighty story,
But is it of defeat or glory?

Do the drops have a preference for their terminal
flight –
In the bright of day or dark of night;
Do they head straight down or settle on window
panes
As a smile would prove that their deaths weren't
in vain.

Taking a Fall

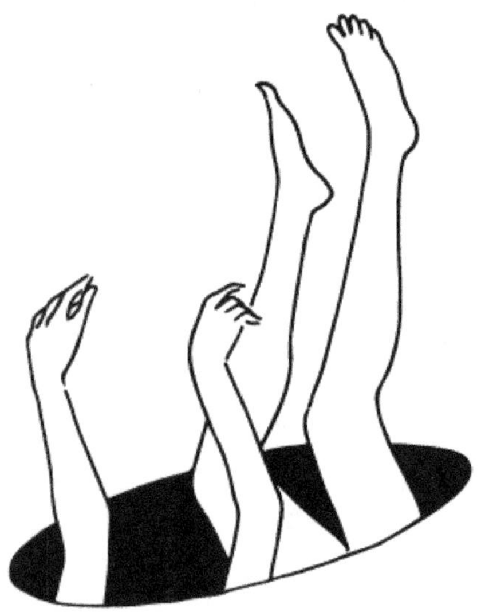

I see you there sulking,
All alone,
Hating reality,
In a different world;
Wishing hard on a distant star.

You watch me come over,
Hide your face,
Saying you're fine but
Avoid my gaze.

You know I'm here, whatever you need,
Don't fret, just follow my lead–

Getting up does it all,
Need to learn how to take a fall,
I know the hurt is not that small.
If you can't, take my hand
I'll teach you how to dance,
Even through the rainfall.

A Stroll Through the Woods by the Ocean Side

A stroll through the woods by the ocean side,
It doesn't get much better than this;
All the secrets that nature confides,
THIS is the truest known bliss!

Walking on a dim-lit path
Amidst Mother Nature's calls,
Hearing and feeling the wrath
Of the Sea upon the rocks.

Here, I have found solace–
Desiring nothing more nor what might be,
Breathing in the salt-laced air,
Lost in the tranquility.

I now stop and look within–
Immersed in the sound of the writhing Sea;
This stroll through the woods by the ocean side
Has, once and for all, SET ME FREE!

Once Upon a Brawl

Things were said, choices made,
Worst of the options laid.
Friendship now turns to hate,
Finally time to bid goodbye.

We knew better, but we were young;
Chalks thrown and accuses flung,
Vows broken and curses hurled,
Now living in separate worlds.

Reminiscing a time of joy
When sunshine triumphed over dark
Just long enough to leave a mark;
Is it possible? From finish to start?

Out of sight but never forgotten.
Eye contact – the stares are rotten.
Each longing to talk, none the wiser
That the other is burning with the same desire.

One fine day, together we yield,
The wound inflicted seems to have healed;
Though we remain wary of such rows to come,
Together is better, and much more fun!

Booked

An escape from reality,
Into a better world;
Better in many ways,
Or so I have learnt.

A doorway with a time limit,
That I open each chance I get,
And fall even more in love
With the ones I shall never forget.

As I read, I empathise,
Their problems – now mine;
A handy evasion indeed,
Though I lose track of time.

Oh, how I wish their world was real,
And that I could call it home,
Their company would be the warmth of a
homecooked meal,
But I know it is foolish to hope so.

If one of them dies,
So does my soul,
Though momentarily, but
Always leaves a hole.

In the midst of all this,
In the back of my mind,
I can hear my parents calling;
Well, isn't that well timed?

Someone That Matters

Saw a little boy today, mourning,
Tears streaming down his face,
Already missing her warmth,
Counting down the days
Until he can see her again.

A grandma is homeliness personified,
If you need toffee, she's the one;
She stops your parents from scolding you,
And scolds them in return!

She knits the warmest sweaters,
And finds the sweetest words,
You can tell her all of your mischiefs
That she'll pretend she's never heard.

As I watched this boy,
My heart shattered,
As I too remember the feeling
Of losing someone that matters
That much.

Still gazing at the boy,
I took a walk down memory lane;
It was pleasant, yet painful,
But beautiful all the same.

Those memories are not erasable,
For a grandmother is truly irreplaceable.
And I know, without doubt, that
This boy will move on and be fine, with time,
Just like I moved on after losing mine.

Marked Difference

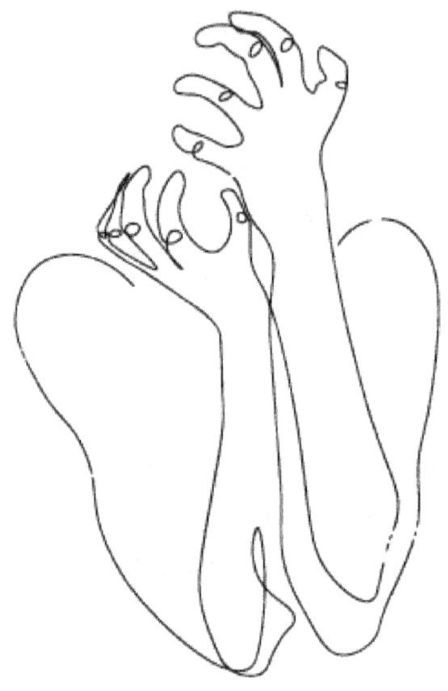

Follow the usual routine–
Eat, sleep, study, repeat;
Got to keep my head buried in my books
Lest they should bury me.

Another meaningless test,
The consequences high;
I'm here doing my level best,
Happy to comply!

Delighted they concluded,
My dragging feet now jump!
Just keep in mind this one thing–
The effort matters less than the outcome.

Don't get worked up, they say,
For you have nothing to fear;
Little do they know of the misery,
The hard work, pain and tears!

God! That's admirable, they say,
An 'almost perfect' score;
If almost was enough, well then
Why isn't it enough for me to soar?

One Year

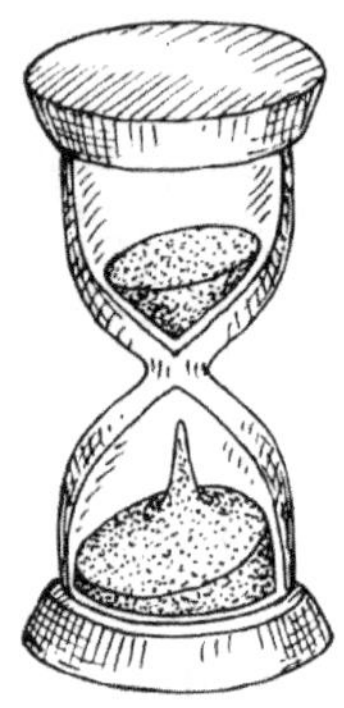

One year is all we had
To make new friendships and memories last,
Got through the joy and sad,
Might have made others feel a little bit bad, but–

These are the days
We get to live our lives,
No need to fret about the when, where and why!

These are the days
Without friends by our side,
Fearless like we'll never ever die!

Bonds we created – fragile as lace.
True love they said, now we laugh in their face.
We wanted it slow, but it picked up the pace,
We never realised – lost in the haze.

All I want is for these days to last
With this set of friends and
Fun I know I'll lack.
No more fights; no more lies,
Not ready to say goodbye.

The Last Time

It's hard to believe
It's the last time we're together,
Sitting on the hard wooden bench,
Searching below for my eraser.
Oh, these days shall never cease to make me
smile;
Now I watch as time gallops–
Leaving me in the dust.
Thinking, how much longer can I make this last?

Because you've been my best friend forever;
You're the main link to my childhood and past.
Will your mind be on me and not on the teacher?
Or will you forget me by the second period?
I know these memories will stick to me like
glue,
Because you're everything to me, and I love you.

The Enigma Wrapped in a Riddle

To live is to love,
Is to laugh, is to cry;
But what is it to die?

An alluring mystery
That has tainted history
Blood red;
Explained by science,
Defied by seance;
Anyway, where are the dead?

Those who claim to know
Are still unsure,
Unable to answer why;
What lies beyond our world?
People are dying to know
The beautiful truth,
Or lie.

This conundrum has stumped many,
I for one shan't waste my pennies
In the hopes of such a breakthrough.
I shall know at the time of death,
Now I lie peacefully in bed;
But, after reading this,
Restless are you.